feel recordings

in the evershift

WAVE BOOKS / SEATTLE & NEW YORK

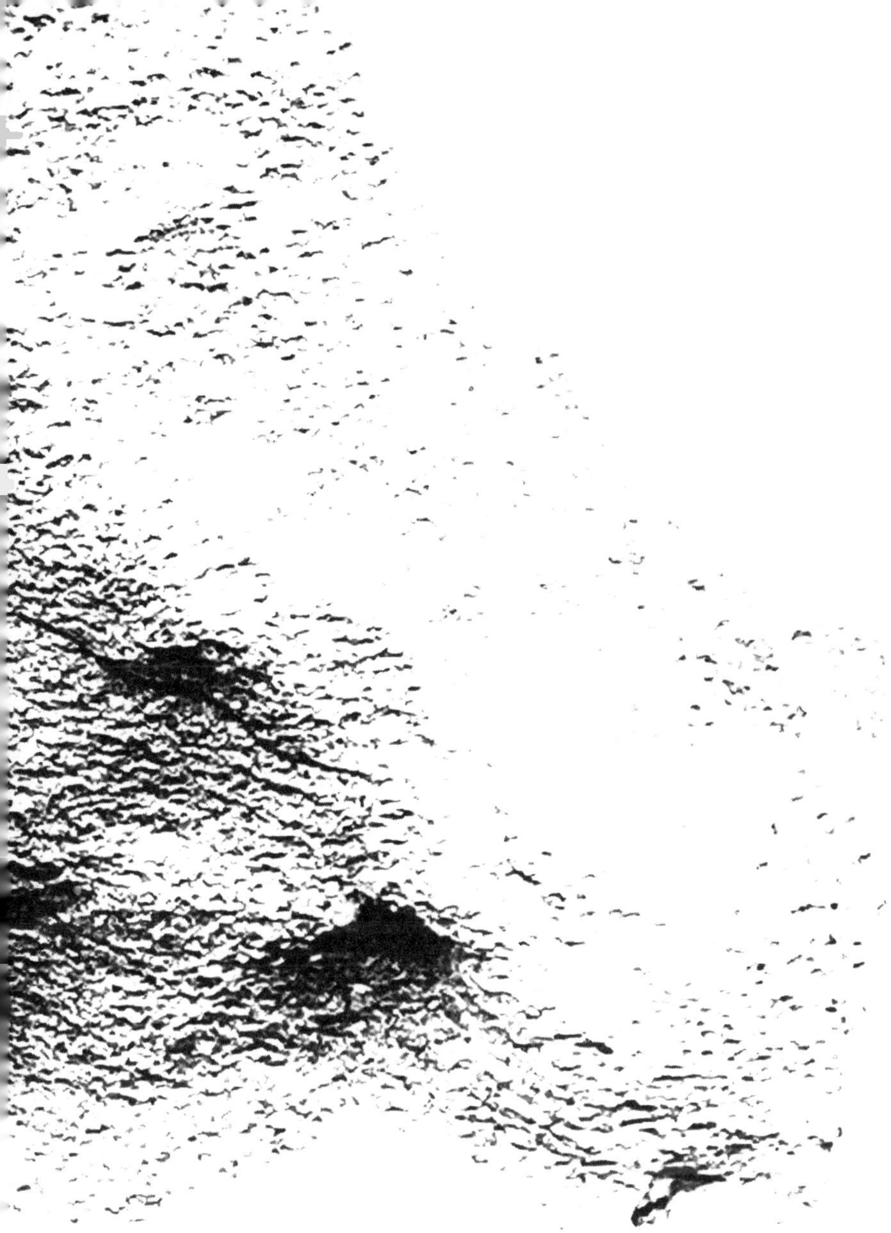

edwin torres

Published by Wave Books
www.wavepoetry.com

Wave Books titles are distributed to the trade by
Consortium Book Sales and Distribution
ipage.ingramcontent.com / (800) 937-8200 / ips@ingramcontent.com
Library of Congress Cataloging-in-Publication Data
Names: Torres, Edwin, 1958– author
Title: Feel recordings in the evershift / Edwin Torres.
Description: First edition. | Seattle : Wave Books, 2026. |
Identifiers: LCCN 2026009867 | ISBN 9798891060487 paperback
Subjects: LCGFT: Poetry
Classification: LCC PS3570.0696 F44 2026
LC record available at https://lccn.loc.gov/2026009867
Designed by Crisis
Photoglyphics on opening and closing pages
and expanse poem on pp. 55–63 by Edwin Torres
Printed in the United States of America
9 8 7 6 5 4 3 2 1
First Edition
Wave Books 130

field

field

field

at the gate of the open sphere

of ancient trees
    of bloods
of *one*—or *else*
    to happen in

stretch out
    the word for
thing—for what means
    thing

of eaters
    bending
breathing—you
    of you

that older lung
    of
you—of *tell*
    of

what re tells
    the wild
of wind—a younger
    tongue

of eating wind
    inside
the wild—the wildest
    of

the eater's *so*
    the lowest light
the centered—*o*
    the eater's ode

of you
    by you
of thing—*re*
    tooled

by *of*
    re read
of—*of*
    re ring

re *you*
    of tell—
—of what means
    tell

to follow the fellow i

for leave us unsettling
save us unsettling—trail us untellable tales

of our settling—fail us our bellowing
harrow'd and hailed by our

failure to follow us—follow the fellow us
trailed in the full of us

fellable follows that see how we orbit our
leave to be full of us—healed in the hollow we

steal what becomes of us—saved what we made of us
sorrowed the soil we surround our unsettling

leave us unsettling—save us unsettling
trail us untellable tales of our settling

fragile ascensions of mayfair and waterbye—
raindow sondaughterbye

painlow some flutter wifi mortal loner
be—lower my lower i

called out of worry i will see to woe was a
fellow to follow i—trailed by the follow i

solo'd the sorrow
to heal what i borrow'd i—came to my sorrow

by—
healing the hollow i

of my mother's mother's mother

of my climate's mother—is my mother's mother   of whose mother—is my
mother's climb   of my father's climb—is my father's mother's mother   of
whose mother's father's brother—is some other sister's mother   of some
other's climb—is my instant climb of my ocean's mother—is my instant ocean's
father   of what distant mother—is my mother's mother's mother   and
what distant ever—is my ever's other father   and my father's distant lover—
of my distant lover's father   of my father's father—is my other's other   and
whose baby—is my baby's ocean—my baby's other ocean   and whose toes—
of my father's distant toes   of my baby's toes—of my lower ocean   of my
golden lower ocean—is my distant ocean's toe   and my older river's woe—
and my river's entered woe   and whose entered soul—is my ever's other soul
and what—is your ever about   your soul about—your inner way to woe
about   and my father's feel'yer faster—is my   failure's faster fall—and my
sky's abundant soul   is my water's tele-motion—is my mother's tele-soul
and my ever's other ocean—and whose waves   are whose ocean—my
ever'ocean—my ever'ed   other'ocean   what—are your waves about—your
ears—what   are your ears about—your earther's ears about—did you   with
those—earther's ears of yours—your ever's ears—about what   you're about—

is here did you—with your water woe—your inner water's woe hear my
seven-layered ocean—with your inner-layered woe my civil after'ocean—
my after'd ocean—did you with your schism inner fauvren—hear my
brethren matre—earthren patre—seethren of my tettle'in—of my fathren—
of my fate'ld others—my 'ethren others—my evil'd other's my ever'ed
mountain'ens—seeth'ren of my mouth'ren—of my face'len's outer water'en
blessed father's moth'ren—blessed outer ressonin' what—is your 'eaven
about—your 'eaven even about—what—is your other about if other—
ever falls—if never ever—falls—of my ever—could ever ever fall of
my—other'en—is my—day'telin—of my cumulu'n—is my—skyttl'in—of
my—seeker'en is—my chroma stay—my chroma hue—sky—stay my—
other sky—stay ever my other of my—herra terra mecca seeker—sayer
sky of my say—sky—stay—sky—stay—sky stay my say'er—my
seek'er—my say'er—my home of my climb—is my home how climbing—
is of home of seres—of sins—of my sorrows of my earthen motre—
otras of my others of others of others—of my ooo'thres—of oth're's—of
oooo's of fath'res—of oth're's—of 'oooo's'ceans of my shunned allevers
of my loves—of my love's—of my o's of my othre's 'orrow's 'oes—of my
imminent ohms—of my—imminent omminent ohms—of my of's of
whose—mother's mother's of's of my—other's other's of's

transfer point

we have crossroads we've known
crossroads that have shown us the way
where we see what passes
for change for wisdom for action
we've seen what lies obscured countless
warnings with need for breathless want
self-fulfilled heroic lights among us
at the outstretched indifference
of mankind our crossroads
paved over by repetition layered
in circumference our prayers will continue
in voices we've heard before
relegated to history by inoculated falsehoods
our transfer points will never fade
bound by fate to repeat lest the repeater
become the fate how nebulous
the deity in charge of the coal house
the driver that dares the crossing its emblem
our breathless horses—the hearts
of our emotive present

to the ekphrastic i

it took that long / in my *seismic* narrative / to layer
my narrative / it took mysterious marvels
of brain to hand / of blood to lung / of obviously fractured air

to walk into *the greater than* / the larger brood surrounding man
it took that long / re-surfacing perception / re-covering sound
to borrow my brood / it took mysterious marvels / of me

let me step into vibration / my porous narrative / what i do
in my writing / to *seismic* my narrative
to cover a surface / by motivating a surface

it took that long / to constantly perceive *surface*
as a cover for *re* / i am a *re* / covering *new* / surfaces *of*
brain to land / i am a / *re* / covering / *new* / surfaces / *of* /

brain to land / it took the action / of fracturing air / to *borrow*
what i *burrow* / it took the action of *borrowing land* / to *burrow brain*
into *brood* / it took the lower case o / into the lower case u

to *burrow* / beneath *borrowing* / i am the layer / placed over myself
using the i / i was given / i am the layer / placed over myself / using the i
i was given / it took *the larger than* / to come from

the larger than / no size am i / no action to i / lower case i / the upper case
belongs to us all / the lower / to me
the newly charged i / seismic borrower / of underground stories

the action of *burrowing* / as *being* / it took obviously fractured broods
to surround obviously fractured i's
it took *earth turner earthworm* / it took *air turner cicada*

it took *water turner beaver* / to become my totems of understanding / to activate
how i borrow / where i belong / how we / *species* / into understanding
to find / where we belong

it took this long / in my life / to arrive here
my totems of *arrive here* / it took that long in my being
to *narrative* my sound / to *narrate* my sound

burial chant: did you in your long life leave any wonder behind

FOR THE NEWBURGH COLORED BURIAL GROUND

• I was 21 and 2 children and 9 years
I was 80 and 22 married years and poverty
I was 27 1 child aged and lived 10 years my senior
I was a bad intemperate and very bad and lived in reputation
    I was 28 and 18 and deserted and sworn and relieved and taken
    I was 10, 4, 7 and deserted
    I was the child of a brown age dependent for 2 years of the above facts
    I was 36 and married and 3 childs and 15 and 8 lived with a husband
•• I was employed and 24 and the youngest sick
I was coal shovel and drived a hack
24 and a wife and pleurisy in the head and 1 child assisted by 1 town
I was 1 mile beyond hope no years no cause
    I was want of a morning
    I was man to no owner no purchase no freedom
    I was 104 yet living all kinds of 77 on 2 tons of coal
    I was soot by the fairy gone wishers of mortals
••• 11 daughters supporting I was living in what I was unable to visit
I was no means assisted near suckle and wand
I was married at 7 unable to 5
I was 4 years of applications left home for another
    I was single and 60 my mother her mother

I was 16 years married and 2 with no lives
I was sick for 3 weeks I was sworn and relieved
intemperate and tamed not able to luster to shine I was made
•••• to be died by a winter
I was father to nothing support for no cause
I was seam to the sick for 1 year at 18 aged 5 and 9 and 31 palsy's
I was color and visit and 50 removed
I was color as long as I could
I was foot frozen switch kept from labor intemperate
rheumatic in service about 20 about 6
I was all about cold I was all about trees
••••• I was 2 at my most at my most about other
I was sworn and relieved I was sworn I was sworn
I was single and aged in vagrant povera
I was born married previously born present consumption
32 about 10 took 7 the elder at 21 aged son
the other emaciated very always in poor
I was 23 and 2 and oldest and sick
I was sick I was sick I was sick I was sick
•••••• I was 20 at 19
a girl of no habit a habit to own
of her residence her reason her rigor her roam
I was youngest a father deserted by age
I was younger a family not able to question
in the town of Montgomery in the town of Parameter
in the town of Volition a seafaring man
••••••• I was 20 yet 40 yet 60 yet some sort of fever
yet married at 19 not able to bed

improvidence delivered a child on its visit
a married arrangement of slaughter and home
    I was 5 without burden a 4 meant to 3
    I assisted a season reseeded by sin
    I was married by 70 and 16 and 1 and of years I was lesser than
    child of no soul
•••••••• made to apply as a lesser than
I was want of a man made of treasure's intemperate
I was previous and former and able and firm
I was taken and little a widower's earn
    a seller's resistance a house on a lot
    I was wife and 2 children and paid for some medicine last week by the river
    28 at 21 I was 4 and then 9
    of 2 years and of 6 40 years and no children
••••••••• I was 12 living 3 months and toes frozen sage
I was 55 years 22 and a barber
unable to labor uncolored by daughter
I was single previously 2 worked visited 16 and found intemperate
    I was 31 towns of a grandchild's demistress
    I was near the creek open to poverty's drink
    I was simple and labor and 12 17 27 on the 20th I was born of supplies
    I was poor of remember
•••••••••• I was bastard to 2 now pregnant by 1
of not sworn was a slave man dead to the years
for 1 year my last I was 1 year alive
about 6 in my pocket for a winter's relent by a chargeable garret I served what I sent
    I was wife of a cook at the village hall bake
    I was wife with the look of a villager's hate

I was 20 consumption was salvage intemperate
a widower's stroke her summer son vagrant
••••••••••• of 18 months leg of not child 45
was a mortgage called mister paid interest on bond
10 years and beg him his grandfather john
and no name was no difference for the offer gone past
I was forest in theft gave provisions to last
a blacksmith by trade 1 of 3 could not tell
any town of assistance of age where they fell
68 19 21 on the plains
•••••••••••• at 14
I was sworn of a sister gone lame
to the amount of her husband both tender and 6 not a cent
owned and left him the lot bought twice
about 12 on the pike
I was application and rumor
I was 47 I was 45 I was 47 I was 45
I was sick I should think
••••••••••••• so deranged no account lately died
and given no previous I was
before I was gone
I was good I was bloom I was stone I was blood I was gone
I was gone
I was law on page 129 at the bottom
I was many years turned by the labor I sought
I was no means of country I was color and caught
•••••••••••••• I was long time deserted some 3 weeks employed
I was wood for the barber I was born of resistance

I was drowned this morning interred by a man
I was found of resistance interred by a land
    interred by indifference
    interred by a mind
    I was punished and 20
    I was waiter and kind

skry is a delicate ocean

my ear—weeps
for a time gone by
or is that what sound does
to the angled tonic

where the *origin you*
what you
you choose—speaks
of *unseen you*

a difficult shun
to speak—of the unseen
is to love
unbearably linguistic

begrowth: i.e. growth

• • •

maybe it's time to convey thought into action
what *mind* does—to the layered *real*
to *blend in* with
to find familiarity—by *blending in* with
to blend into *layer*
removal of *the*—that is—*the* layer
what *the* does—to unknown shaping
—*the*—unknown shaping
of every new listen
to record—in earthbound readings
emblems that point
towards—earthbound readings
that bring—into *here*
what *mind* does—to *into*—as a way to understand
—what interrupts

• • •

trans-poetic immersion—structures
that evolve
out of *needs*—to survive
—*what do you need to survive*—
take *new* out of *need*
—what day's equilibrium

does to *new*
—*the* new—
that operate *underskin*
where *mind* is inserted
—*the* here—
that want to be heard
minutiae into *new*—emanating
from *underknown*
—all that 'n' emanating as *nnnn*—into *new*
how *nnnn*
starts as *knoooownnn*
and who *ownnnns*
without all that—*nnnn*
getting in the way
—*nnnnnnnnnnnnnnnnn*
th'way
of balanced imperfection—
—where *of* operates

• • •

for the *known* to become *dictation*
listen to the unknown
—*become*—
to dissect *line*—out of *imbalance*
what unknown
towards—*want* of *not here*—do you own
—do you want
not here
more than i—or is it

—other way ’round—
dear *known*
use *of*—as immersive zygote
dear *of*—what repeating gesture
of *want*
brings *mind* to *not*
if *not here* is the goal
—when *here* is so comfortable—
is *uncomfort* the goal

• • •

use *of*—as immersive *be-goal*
the opposite of familiarity
begets *instinct*
be-comfort—in the reach of *be-new*
the new goal—the *being*
of goal—*I wanna be the wanna*—
to blend into—the unknown
into—to *blend*
in operation of *instinct*
to *understand*—what *mind* does
—as *climax* of indifference—
how to parse information
for something—*anything*
connected to change
would that—could that
—be
morning of a *thought-in-progress*—or
process of a *morning-in-thought*

• • •

—*transmission*—comes to mind
—what is mind
but blend—i.e. *core* i.e. *new*

—to *core* existence—
the adding of
the

—as a way of being
the *action* you accept—i.e. *to be the wanna*
you wanna be—the *finding* of the familiar

—i.e. to face what is bound to present
—i.e. what is new
—i.e. growth

what mind does to i.e. growth
—what is i.e. growth
but blend

what is—understanding
of growth
but—*life made new by blend*—

the underskinned observation
that won't let go
—before you do

the process or instance of definition

to almost catch—
just passing by—to pass

on the sidewalk—not
about belonging seems

waiting—underneath
a city hideout—

of the good samaritan—
that the one person

in a city of so many—
this city I love

to be—the one chosen
the one flower picked—

for the perfect date
outside the door—

standing guard—
by the perfect eye

the tripping person
the almost fallen
the selected pigeon—limping
the street—the poem
out of place
when it mentions—where it belongs
a 3-story brownstone
a wounded pigeon
to have caught the eye
the chances of that—in this city
who would save it
would see it—who saves animals
to have caught—that eye
that pigeon I don't
this donut
from the party box
for the perfect bouquet—held
by the perfect boy
finding—a wounded distraction
of the perfect ending
holding—the chosen bouquet
over the one pigeon—caught
of the one samaritan—making
the right call

to the one friend—
for most any imperfect

in its chosen nature—
for wounded pigeons

the feathered fall—
the good samaritan rings

caught—by the wounded
the animal's eye—

from street level
of a most perfect man—

suggesting—the correct solution
situation
placing—the wounded animal
a home
found—where there is no nature
by the exact call—the almost person
just before
the chosen door—the perfect drop found
in this exact writing
witness
the pigeon being—the one
who saw me
telling this story
passing by

generosity of a powerful gesture

it is the words' finding of time
and settling
on you

and moon what morning does
clemescent run
across a smear

fact elevates intention no matter
your tossed pillow
the mark you want disappeared

is the one I know you by
still
the ash finds a way from hand to skin

does it implicate
curiosity
to think this way

to trouble a boy
out of a day
to air out an open skull

there's an [ass]ent in my [axx]ent

i wanna live inna—don't wanna live inna / Ah-ah-ah
i wanna rhythm—to live inna rhythm a / Me-eh-eh
i wanna live inna—infinite inner / Rica-ah-ah
pity the pattern of—po-po-po-poems / 'at try to belong

can you
seek or forsake a facade
if you
keep a compassionate palm
could your
infinite ever evolve
if your
liminal ever re-co-coco

my anthropology—your loco
minor lobotomy—your yoyo
my 'pistemology—your uh oh
my weaponology—flow

it's the > *Romeo > Julio > ba • rri • o •*
how do we > leave it no > bo • dy • know •
quita pa' > tra, Fibo > na • cci, • bro •
do it and do it and • do it and do it and • do it and do it • again

to the
seeker deceiving a soul
can you
rica the mecca for gold
for the
keeper to sever the po-ethnic
seek it or leave it alone

why vivify a revival—i
tried a recital in high school—i
played a malevolent bi-fool—i
did it because of my name

i spoke a reversible accent—from
better to badder to good—both
officer KRUP and a SHARK—i played
both in the guise of a hood

que pasa mi-versible axis
su casa mi casa my guess is—i
learned how to pirouette optics
a movie Boricua was i

ever re-open the - ri
- o
ever re-sever the - mi
- o
ever re-barrier - bar
- rio
ever the rebel -
- the we

toca mi lengua de vo / ca-ca
musica boca pa'tra / la-la
never la cuca la'ra / cha-cha
got it we get it / let's go

i wanna live inna—don't wanna live inna / Ah-ah-ah
i wanna level—a lower rebellion a / Meh-eh-eh
i wanna live inna—minimal inner / Rica-ah-ah

i wanna live inna liminal center
i wanna live inna liminal center
i wanna live in the limitless enter
i wanna live in the limitless enter

mad dementia in little italy

8 Nuyorican Abuelitas … Walk into an Italian restaurant
Grand Mamá Nonna its name … 8 Chinese Grandmothers
And one Italian Man … Walk to their table … Their daily walk
8 Beast Feeders … Walk into an Italian Grandmother … *Grandma Mamán*
8 Chinese Breast Walkers … Walk into a marble bust
Wearing ivory capuchin fatigues … *Please sir for today the special*
8 Bull Walkers storm a village … Running with stationary policemen
Pamplona's money shot … To choke on voyeurs
Thrown into the lion's mouth … 8 Tourists in a coal mine
8 Social Contortionists … Ripped out of Algorithm's Trifecta
8 Cautionary Vibrators set on stun … 8 Facial Distortionists … 8 Bolivian Tarantulists
Ready for silent protest … In togas of Old World morality
Walk into an Italian tourist trap … Little is not a country
But a neighborhood … Disguised as a nation
In a size … To soften the blows of ethnic cleansing
8 Mountain Goats … Walk into an Italian restaurant
Grandmamá Mamámamá Mamámamá Mamámamá
How is please sir everything? … Terrific thank you
Buongiorno! … Master Waiter praises descent on his enemies
While returning to the kitchen … Glancing at the cloven despair
Of dark alley day jobs … 8 Godless Pharaohs
Commit afternoon faux pas for a Chinese Bookie
The continent Rubik'd … In a game of lunch specials
For demagogues and gangster chefs … The culture wars

Were never this close ... On my third-grade map in the Bronx
One town over from China ... 8 Saint Gennaros ... Walk into a street fair ...
NoNó NoNoNoNó NoNoNoNó Mamá Mamamamá Mamamamá
8 Italian Grandmothers ... Will steam your shirt
All subtlety and dashiki entendre ... Left intact
8 freshly unwrapped Italian Implants ... Walk into a Chinese business meeting
Ready for slaughter ... Lasagna Bolognese and Peking Duck ... On one plate
8 Mouth Feeders will get the check ... If you spread your dime
In a downtown dive ... That knows your name

herald a mythic word

a folding—by sail
a way of winding—through one letter
one cryptic signifier—out of gesture

a shorn advance
a plight—out of venture
the risen crevice—formation of a soul

endures its mold
if images—could speak
what one—might hear

for some a glitch
to crattle the romantic itch—were *itch*
a turn

finner reek *obtainer*
stirs a human—an early *remainer*
to call off a settling—using *if*

as a wand
as if—*hands*
could lessen yours

here *co*

or *go*—as *teeter* to *edge*

as *take* to *seer*

such *con*—to *co*

haven neck—twill

twitched hair—on *strick encrounted*

will you—my myth

ally styer—gull wretch

all off—flayed off

as *if*

to *slay*—were *co*

to *pair*

trellescent trail

solid mass
in wake light   makes *form*
            —and meets us

            awakes
            our massive *us*
                        —aurored

                                    in dusted   full luna
                                    prey   in moated
                                                —pure ruin

            by omni-heaven rail
            perfected
                        —preempted   informed immover

                                    half-seed taker
                                    rakes me   raw
                                                —renders *make*

its name   its wake
takes fleet
            —to line along   trellescent trail

to sky alone
to leave
—in solid light
against
—ennui
you leap
ascorched
—in scrawl

abyss enters the conversation

feathered serpent heart of sky
    what does pushback do
to inner calm
    which cliff to claim as yours

chromic integer
    how quick does your entropic rosary
frame familiarity with survival
    what i wish for *self*

is to see what *self* allows
    the year i became
explicitly intimate
    as the neck i stroked

a thread appeared
    as a sheet of glass
against the shards i seek
    my own oblivion *gorgeoused*

by those before me
    abyss enters the conversation
who is unreal
    to the pain they feel

the unknown hold
    of their inner psalm
who am i to dare unreal
    the world unreal

lost my step
    go ahead, abyss was talking

as if the ending of quiet … were my percussive element
my ending and quiet in this world
as if ending and quiet … were percussion
emerging into shape
my world … my shape
out of what seems to be … my next shape
my final shape … this world
emerge with me

∘ ∘ ∘

as if life were lived intact … and didn't know
it was not finished
as if the continuing … of not being finished
were what life was leading towards
what we … breathe into
what we … percuss into
as if our known next … were in truth
our known unknown

∘ ∘ ∘

as if waves could mimic … the cliffs we were from
as if one shoreline

were enough of an edge ... to climb
to track ... where we've already been
what has always been ... our edge
could cover the world
as if truth ... were a shape we could mimic
a mimic to climb

○ ○ ○

my percussive elements ... of ending and quiet
my pulse against yours
could cover the world ... emerge
my surface ... with me
in the fragment of two
a third
between
the between fragment

○ ○ ○

as if a third fragment ... the one between
were breath ... in breath
as if a third fragment ... the one between
were motion ... in motion
this shoreline ... always
you ... always
in ... always motion
always ending ... there is time

° ° °

in the fragment of soon
you
are the fragment in soon
not the landing
nothing settles
how far . . . before
soon
is now

° ° °

as if what we say . . . were a fragment of saying
a truth . . . a shape
between us . . . a third shape
us
as if now . . . the saying of now
were a distant truth . . . emerge my surface
as if distance . . . were listening
to the ones . . . that call us

° ° °

could hear . . . distance unraveling
what happens . . . when we let in
what happens
between fragments . . . my edge

to yours … how far from us

do we keep

saying … what we say

my quiet percussion … of saying nothing

○ ○ ○

so many fragments … on one spot

so much … on top of much

each of you … in one fragment

who I am … between a third

on this edge

as if one spot

on one shoreline

could cover the world

field

túmba la caña jibarito

Fieldworker: ***takes hard work, my father's be-father / to turn your soil***
my younger's be-younger / to sync your psyche, my other's be-other
to solo your path

Chorus: túmbala poeta
túmbala the mind
túmba l'undulating
lenguas you can't find - am -

Poet: i / the other if
you're / a -
live - are
you / the other am -
i the i

Chorus: túmbala poeta
túmbala palabra
túmbala promesa
túmbala mañana
tryin' to be the people
'tween a border - isn't
tryin' to free the people
'tween a former word - can you -

Poet: switch / your English
tongue / to
drum - the
glitch / you finish the
fissure's son

Chorus: symbolize d'vision
symbolize d'cision
symbolize a'vision
symbolize i'gnition
túmbala cañita
túmbala casita
túmbala palmera
túmbala fascista
túmbala poeta
campa no'isaida
túmbala yoricua
yunca la compay - do -

Poet: i / portray the
why / you
fear - do
you / forsake the -
why - you hear

Fieldworker: ***gonna swing m'machete / sing a'zucar man field / gonna shine m'forever***
sing a'zucar man field / gonna blind m'forever / sing a'zucar man field
gonna find m'forever / sing a'zucar man field

Chorus: túmbala palabra
sí sí - voca'seeker
túmba'mericana /
sí sí sí - the higher
túmbala poeta
sí sí sí - the ride
túmba l'undulating
lenguas you can't hide - your -

Poet: mind / a field your
rise / a
fight - your
light / among a
million lives

Chorus: túmbalize a lingo
lingualize arrival
túmbalize a people
lingualize a right
túmbala poeta
túmbala palabra
túmba jibarito
túmbala all night - but i -

Poet: got / to go i
got / to
glide - on
my / erasure

one more time - i leave / you
with this
one more / high - in the -
grand / *we* of
things / we
choose - do we
stand / to *be* of
things - we lose

weave ender

say on *do*
on *and on*
say on moonar
intelligence
lace
of
cloud
goldens
the
iral

one
month
of
day
calibrates
same
month
of
day

how far from each *does each want*

these quit texts are anti-fissure reality

I am asking about form and foam
And surface and mass
I am asking how people decide
Who fissures—who assembles
Who listens already assembled

Who in their previous seeking
Let your seeking—find theirs
Who was finger—who was river
Who left you alone
I am asking who sat on the moon in one life

To say it was none
Who gave you your heart
Who let you roam—I am asking
Who are the people—doing—at the same time
Impossible immensity

Who interjects—slide reality—with
Sword infinity—word reality
A poet's agility—to enter agility
Who gave you your ears—who loosened your rust
Who is anti-possible I am asking

- *Mannequin ectophan*
- *Stictuc inker*
- *Man ec*
- *Mam es*
- *Nan ec*
- *Man ex-static*

Just some surfaces to explain how I got here
How life sustains philosophy
Over deep fake
Who propels deep fake—who gave you
Deep fear as reality

Quit as reality
Who quilted kick—these click bytes are reality
Bits of stream
Paltry accomplishments
Loose associations

For quickly
Moving on from what hurts—these words
Just loose associations
For moving on from what hurts
Who took surprise out of the ether

And gave you a list of wrong turns in the vacuum
Who gave you—your scatter

In the story you choose
Who gave you fear—as a hardship to follow
Who cut you off—from the difference you own

I am asking what happens
To the letters unwritten—by the fingers
Unswiped across earth
Who gave you paper and ink and things—that used to say
What was writing and what was holding

Who drained your elegies—and called them light
Who studied your giving
To always conform to the given
Go on—glint affirmation for pleasure
Who gave you patterns to continue

Where *start*—where *end*
Where *choose*—there is—no *who*
To the pattern
I am screaming my way out of an empty room
Subverting *the oetic*—to understand

How there is nothing to understand
Who gave you witness—and called it quit
Who gave you *One Way*—and *Right Way*
When clearly—*No Way*
Does fear have light in the anti-possible

I am asking about an empty room
That doesn't know—how to finish
Who gave you an empty room
I am asking—about volume and distance
And who fissures—who foams

invocation for the freefall

(WHEREIN THE FOURTH BEGETS THE THIRD)

how best to observe the infinite in-progress
but gratitude   my gratitude for fleshly remaining
for orbiting santatia   alive in sensual vertigo
my framing release   as form untouched

I am not healed or in space   but as I am
I am not broken or in motion   but there again
I am not bramble or volume   but face folly
at the worry of intimacy

I dive back into freefall
gazing in all directions   to land
begotten by freefall
and how to be grateful for the fold

of lenticular light pods   of empty sail
as imploding oracle   of denser replacements
the learned unknown
as broken chamber   my heart as explosion

shrapnel divination   devolving isolation
eternal by arrival   and how to thank perception

of spirits I ascend through
I long for awareness of the eternal

I long for the faces I share out there
I long for the narrow strip the unmeasured walk
and what brings such dearness to closeness
and all fragile warmth to ecstasy

and feral speed speeder my fast my faster
I thank perception of the spirits the friends I don't contact
to have known such improbable alignment
the animals I don't see I thank the family I don't have

the ones I do the objects I live
the lives I've loved what is it
that burrows beneath perception of the immaterial
but freefall wasn't it—gazing
above as below and how to reignite
the quivering mainframe I relish
aroused by arrival—those *r* words
delicious for the rose'd flesh

the standing unseen previousness
that allowed *here* to happen emotional gratitude—my green
my open window
the thing I'm so *thing* at
elegy of my most distant voice

and our hands as humans
and farewell the express
and you my bothness
my lazy I haver

the thing that's coming isn't the thing here
the thing broken
metonymic interior thing I can't touch
the thing I'm not worried about
what I hold on to

the burbling criterion I'm not about

I thank perception of the rise—then again
ahead of itself—the step
the choosing the catch derelict traveler
self-nomad of selves
selv'er—they'er—you'er
isolated creature
weaving interstitial enigma

I'm not choosing—*ever* as the most—actual
but—*freefall*
as cosmic interior
the mosaic opens
—and how does the same
unfold

the enormous expanse of
what it takes to make a day →

• the *other* — becoming — the *other* — is the page — rooted by language

the *other* — becoming — the *order* — is definition — at play

the *other* — becoming — is the poem — rerouted

to the tumble of *order*

the making

of *field*

• page is feel

to the incomplete empowered

where *edge*

absorbs expectation

• page is turn

• where *turn* is perception as journey

• fraught with incompletion — forging safety in the incomplete

• page is incomplete

• to raw movement —using *turn* as language —shifting endlessly with arrival

• page is arrival

position *activates* position

i to i

alignment as i

• receiver is alignment

where to situate *self-speak*

within

tangible action

• just tell me what you're thinking

• to meet other *lifebloods* — to tumble *external* — to harvest *inner lingual*

• *set within field*

• *is field*

• *i field*

• just tell me what you field

eomantic arrangement for a wolf star

expansive
the solo
of an eonic landscape
to spark
one sparticle
to speak
one spark

slight return

how do i entangle my dismemberments
the richly detailed confusions i embody
for a go at free

maybe respect is harnessed out of tyranny
the self-aware protagonist
inched by frame

notepad as digital implosion
how do i form my thumbs
to catch the flames enslaved

by songs from other poems
how does that *re-embered* memory
creep the active same

matters of release have nothing to do
with what we have
but what we move through

these restless times i conjure
tuned into a fragility
that i can't imagine aligns with mine

the writing of animals

○ ○ ○

[*what animals you, what wants you*]

I had animals lined up . . . to smell yours . . . I once had similar creatures
but I was a different tone . . . I once put strokes to stride . . . but I was a different
sort of dog . . . I once had gills at the side of my testaments . . . but I was
a brilliant miscreant . . . I once had scent as an available orifice
but it was someone else's skin . . . I let fall . . . someone else's ocean
I let in . . . someone else I could not imagine

I once wanted so badly
to feel everything—that I let go
of my world—to let it happen

I once knew the travel of my sweat
would unleash a tremor
so far beyond my sight—that I held onto perception
beyond my skin—to let it happen

I once needed affirmation's reminder
with such feral acuity—that I let go
of my size—to let it happen

I once thought ferocity wanted me for mobility
with so many centers revolving—that I smelled the spot
at the scratch of my back—to let it happen

I once allowed myself the walking through
of an air so dense with temporal serenity—that I held on to registers
incomprehensible to acute attenuations of interlingual
arousal—to let it happen

I once telegraphed my tremor to the sacrum before the cortex
with such badass delivery—that I let go of a torment I'm only now
understanding was deeply sown to my twinned removal
of seed and sift—to let it happen

I once reasoned balance as solitary right
with such baring of self—that I transitioned
into tension—to let it happen

I once wanted so thoroughly to know
whether I could attract the subtlest domains
of sensory arousal—that I stoned my hide

entranced by delineation
the animal perceives—and lets it happen

∘ ∘ ∘

[***what spots you, what traps you***]

I *wanttianimal* **you** *tenear* **you** I *mananimal* I *want* **you** *tihearne* I
want **you** *tocatchmenottoseemetolet migoinyourtrapimananimal*
I *want* **you** *toletmecatch* **you** *toletmehearmesee* **you** *imansee* **you**
I *wanttianimal* **you** I *wanttoseehow* **you** *hearmewhen* I *catch* **you**
sittinginthedarsittingwhere I *dontdar* **you** *butsee* **you** *inthehear* **you**
imadarkadarhol I *wantto* I *wantti* **you** *mak* **you** *sit* **you** *mak*
you *hearyi* I *manhear* **you** I *wanttointomysee* **you** I *manimal* **you**
tosee **you** *sit* **you** I *masit* I *wanttosit* **you** *myseetohear* **you** *makmesee*
you *makmehear* **you** *makmewalkrightbythehinterthehuntertryinttocatch*
you I *wattocatchthhuntertryinhtocatch* **you** *fasterthanmyhearin*
cantypecancatchthesewords fastrthamytipsmytrips **you** *intokingdos*
thdarkestintokingdon I *gaveof* **you** I *thedarkextcave* I *gacewasmykingoyofhearomy*
sittingspot I *mahuntedspot rryomgtocatchyourhearingof* I *thehearingof*
mycachingisan ecnotendingtohunthuntingmyending isahearinggatchthswords
fastrthn I *cancaththeclosinhofthscave* **you** *theexitofthisdeepesthearin*
isahumted cavetohumthrough tomurmurthrough I *mamurmrunghunted*
amuoofmisundeftsnfing ogagreementmis agreementofunderstanging
I *wanttostandunder* **you** *anhuntyouragreesivehearingtocallmeththings* I
wanttoheardbythethngs I *wanttovecalledby* **you** *letthemthrowmeout*
letthemtellmeitstimetogo etthemhumtterownagreementofmishearing
anthrowmeoutwhentheexitispresentelefttoright etthemtellmeitstie
toleavemyhearing isinagreementwith **you** *yoursittingwiththesitting*
ofalthesehearsthearts allthesecandlesdimybreatheduponmycatching
thedinofwhat I *want* **you** *todowithme quisatonewiththethousands*
thatcamebeforemethesteps I *creakedwhen* I *leftbeforemiletthmthrow*
meoutanretirntothedin thlovelyimmersionofthings I *willneverhearbutbe*

○ ○ ○

[*what I have for you, what arrived for you*]

To consider *earth* as *arrival*—for words to gravitate towards, to settle on timelessly gorgeous derelicts of language, to settle on the flotation devices wrapped around the layered actions that define change—what will our words do to change the earth—with the places we visit, with our language, with considerations of placing, with how we own our landings—what will the motivation for ending—do—to change our ending, to land or maybe, only, arrive—in action of supple ability, to the human body—not compliant, not flexible, not allowed until told so—the human mind, is a place inside earth, told to be earth—to be the human, telling the mind to arrive—its own planet, the human arrival—not pliant, until given words to assemble around, to land—with gentleness, the force needed for change.

To strike familiarity, in consideration of arrival—of earth as arrival, in consideration of alphabet—to allow integers of cryptic consideration, their translation, for creatures of cognition, to absorb intention, to allow, of place—the human earth, its roam—for giving place, what we do, with time—inside earth, to mine through human change, the consideration for change—to note, how long it takes to set out, what words do, to ignite the human, out of the human—to arrive as a fuse, to note the implosion, of speech—as arrival, and how it affects our human mind—to consider the mind, as a place, to allow layered action, its depth, complicit depth—to arrange notions of human complexity, as mistake-filled *prones*—to own our *prones* to action, to be prone to action and assemble abilities, as triggers, to use speech that implies friction, as a need for change—to know, that change is action out of reversal, out of what triggers implosion to ignite evolution—by writing, in ways that don't arrive easy.

Unaccustomed to being caught—the human mind is not earth, is not alphabet—is not a stranger to words, as a place for landing—unaccustomed to stagnant episodes of hierarchy—the human earth is not a stranger to evolution, to the redone resonance of false implications—the human earth, in mind, to the mirrored imperfections of the rendered obsolete—the human earth, in mind, to the chosen arrival, a disguise of arrival—to the rusted ladder, a blending wall—to the manufactured escape of the human spirit, the construction of place, as consideration for landing—to apprehension as sport, for the human mind—to barriers invented, unaccustomed to spirit—to words that absorb intention, by reframing ability, as punctuation liberators—of earth as liberty, in face of spirit—to allow human arrival its place—by reframing place, to gravitate towards change, by reframing change—to set out timelessly, the human earth, as a mind—in consideration of arrival.

○ ○ ○

[***what exits you, what exists you***]

I don't know how to tell you
that I'm scared of losing what I have
that my brain is a sieve and this body
has I don't know how much longer
and that I need to know that my all
was not in vain my words how I see
my world was not for nothing
so I have to keep writing what I imagine
will connect to somewhere I've been
already that I've never seen somewhere

that doesn't recognize everyone but me
how easy to say I'm not as strong as you
that I need to know how everything I did
was worth something and then that means
to who who is the large ideal that will
strike me who is the outside myself that
I'm charging towards who else should it be
but right here my own blood who else
but here is who I should listen to

○ ○ ○

[***what serves you, what saves you***]

It is in *fracture* where emblems of humanity set root, where the initial stages of cognition assemble nerve endings, to create, from that which remains. The semblance of thought, in its origin as flesh—is manifest by the reception of flesh, in its perception as thought. To envision *fragment* as a whole, is to embody *fracture* as immersion.

This is language taking root in fracture. The form of that fracture is what poetry allows for—to raise questions, among the detritus of alphabets that humans survive on. If poetry is an animal in the landscape of our bodies, the question of the animal is to survive our truth, to call on our fractured forms to save us.

Here now, the repetition of *mark-making*, where *self* finds *self* between selves—before arrival of *same* self as *other* self—before departure of *same* edge, core of *be*, in edge—before *same* edge, defining *self*, as human *other*—selfing in *constant self*, off *guttural bounce*, is *other*—this is fracture taking root.

Same flesh—says stroke, appears as vertical affiliation with breath—

says body between arrivals, where fracture finds human. Where endings interrogate—what thought does to cave, what mind does to flesh. What gathers, as form, the fracture's immersion.

I've exhausted my powers of observation—here now, the concreteness of the body.

◦ ◦ ◦

[***what marks you, what glyphs you***]

A line crossed along two faded slants
A series of curved fingers around the base of a square, the edges becoming points on a horizon of stars
A secondary smudge behind a torn window
A shadow's incision drawn across a v-shaped bear
A tiny bonsai trunk with razor leaves twisted in the shape of a boat
A rectangle reaching out at the edge so that its center is an imploded mountain obscured by a tornado
A heart with tiny limbs attached to each bump
A streak smoothed out over a chocolate-looking cloud
A small face without lips
A flotation on faraway skin that sits next to you as you turn your head to face me
A timepiece forgotten by each hand, its numbers a circle of scars arranged by perspiration
The shadow of a reflection before its arrival
A fish crevice attracted to the ground
A violin-shaped bird with a beak where its wings should be
A kiss looking for more

A sky in the cleft of your lips
A spell I could lose myself in
A forest of trees in the palm of my hand
The profile of a cubist bargain
A tidal wave scattered by a mosquito's wake
A sideways view of an alien's haircut
The number twelve before it becomes thirteen
A ring replaced by a finger
An elephant sitting still before it arrives
The wriggling tail of a snake
A flame over a cross
A wandered road along the side of a whirl
A u-shaped ear along four seedlings
Scattered freckles outlining a wrinkle
A splinter caught on a wing
A fern pressed between erroneous moons
A clipped closeness bent along three slips
A cradled whisper by peach fuzz
The hum of hair along the neck
A grip at the small of your back
The carbon of an eclipse
A shape in the mouth of a world
A gash pretending to be
Two dots following five more
A rivering stripe along the edge of a sea
A polar bear looking for home
A crescent cave with a horseshoe on top

my ankle
my thumb
my wrist
my forearm
my eyebrows
my lower calf
my belly
my knuckle
my elbow
my palms
my right hip
my left wrist
my nose
my inner thigh
my middle toe
my neck
my kneecap
my lower back
my right shoulder
my ear
my chest
my underarm
my earlobe
my temples
my sacrum
my chroma
my solar plexus
my pinky
my xi

my foot
my left kidney
my breast
my nipple
my thumb
my chin
my lower ribs
my stomach
my cheek

○ ○ ○

[***what I've seen, what I've sinned***]

I saw, off a tree
on one leg, caught by moving pic
I saw, digital, by pixel, by grammar
left alone, by sun
aware, of its impression, on sky
by sky, aware of its impression, on me
I left, what I saw, alone
for its living, to be
sought by me, to give
to what, I can't foresee
to explain, am I allowed, to ask
what it is, to see
in a range, of livingness
re-seen as tree

and then time, as integer
relearns, my see
in a system of roots
so deep, so sent
by too many sendlings, so rounded
by livingness
in warm, of warmth
and then, to leave
my many endings
in time, taken, to align my t's
letters, forcepted
to touch each other, to have made, each other
to be, each word I touch
to see

what it is, I be
one living sun, aghast
on me, agrown, agusted
breath
a given thing, a and
a the, a be
to wait
underneath, a living waitingness, alive
in waiting, with warmth, at my wait
what time says, to wait
what time
fills me with
agated echo, a here
a here

○ ○ ○

[***what reframes you, what encounters you***]

I am a reframed container of continuity
until the next day opens—with further episodes of continuity

it's easy to dismiss a stain
as a discoloration—when given a human filter

folding realities into perceived realities
the point is a compass—and my direction is you

this fact is most important to know
that you are there with me—until the next day opens

our separations—contained
by how we arrange our boundaries

divergent systems
to replicate—what moves inside

I am a binary episode
conditioned—by discoloration

I am in the furthest episode of continuity—morally engaged
to comment on time on space—letter by letter

this gathered assemblage of oracles—the multiple structures
of what we say with what we do—implies continuity

    you were there before me—or was I
    before you, here—fold with me

approach *movement* as—*communion with boundary*
I am a family of boundaries

    here, speaking to you—of ways we leave each other
    to step into new ways of leaving—of ways

we don't speak to each other—when we step into
new ways—of speaking

    right there, before you—the ancient patterns of our texture
    what we reveal—to the edges we crease

the layers of encounter—we arrange
for each other—the about to be moment

    reframed—by the move
    to the space—we commit

    ○ ○ ○

[*what arrived for you, what I have for you*]

in consideration of place, inside earth
of earth, as a place for enders
to gravitate, to conjure, timelessly gorgeous
derelicts of language, to settle
in the flotation devices, wrapped, around our crossings
around layered actions, that define change

what will our words do
to change earth, what will the places we visit
with language, with landing our language, with considerations
of placing our landings, what will the motivation
of ending, of our ending, do, for change
to actually, land

in action of supple ability
the human body, is not pliant
until told so, the human mind, a place
inside earth, until given words
to assemble around, to land with gentleness
the force needed for change

to strike familiarity, the alphabet
allows the animal, its integers of cryptic
consideration, their translation
for creatures of cognition
to absorb intention, to allow, of place
the human earth, its roam

for giving place, what we do, is what we know
to arrive, the human
into the human
with time, inside earth, to mine
through human change, consideration
for change, to note, how long it takes
to set out, what words do

ACKNOWLEDGMENTS

My gratitude to Joshua Beckman for his unwavering guidance throughout the journey of this book's many evolutions.

• • •

The following pieces have appeared in the following publications: "to follow the fellow i," *Poetry Project Newsletter*; "mad dementia in little italy," "skry is a delicate ocean," *Brooklyn Rail*; "begrowth: i.e. growth," *About Place Journal*; "primascape," *Vestiges*; "túmba la caña jibarito," Poem-a-Day, *Academy of American Poets* online.

"the writing of animals" is an excerpt from the chapbook *The Animal's Perception of Earth* published by DoubleCross Press.

"burial chant" was commissioned by the artist Jean-Marc Superville Sovak for an exhibition on the Newburgh Colored Burial Ground at *Ann Street Gallery*, Newburgh, NY.

"of my mother's mother's mother" and "primascape" were written for *Soon Is Now*, a climate festival in Beacon, NY, produced by Eve Morgenstern.

Two grants supported the writings and audio recordings that became core elements in the conception of this material: an Individual Artist Commission from Arts Mid-Hudson (made possible with funds from the New York State Legislature and administered by Arts Mid-Hudson), and a Support for Artists grant from NYSCA sponsored by Bowery Arts & Sciences (made possible by the New York State Council on the Arts with the support of the Office of the Governor and the New York State Legislature).

• • •

And thank you to the fellow i's who lit openings for me through their support, collaboration, and continual inspiration: Sita Chay, Victor Hernandez Cruz, Ram Devineni, Ricardo Gallo, Bob Holman, MC Hyland, Didac P. Lagarriga, Sean G. Meehan, Ariana Reines, David Rothenberg, Gryphon Rue, Joelle Stille, Bradbury Thompson, Stephen Vitiello, Anne Waldman, Alex Waterman, and Elizabeth & Rubio.

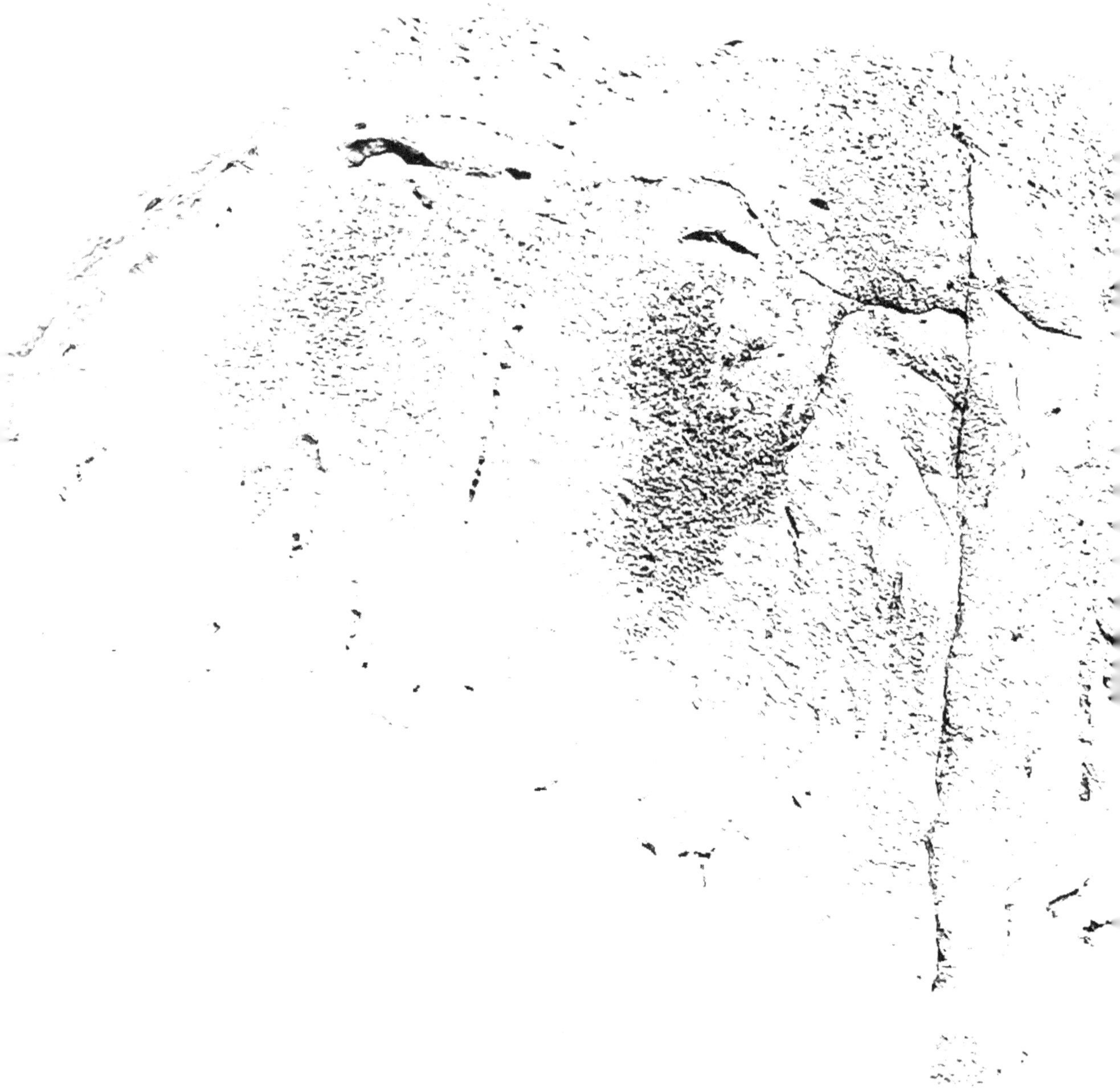

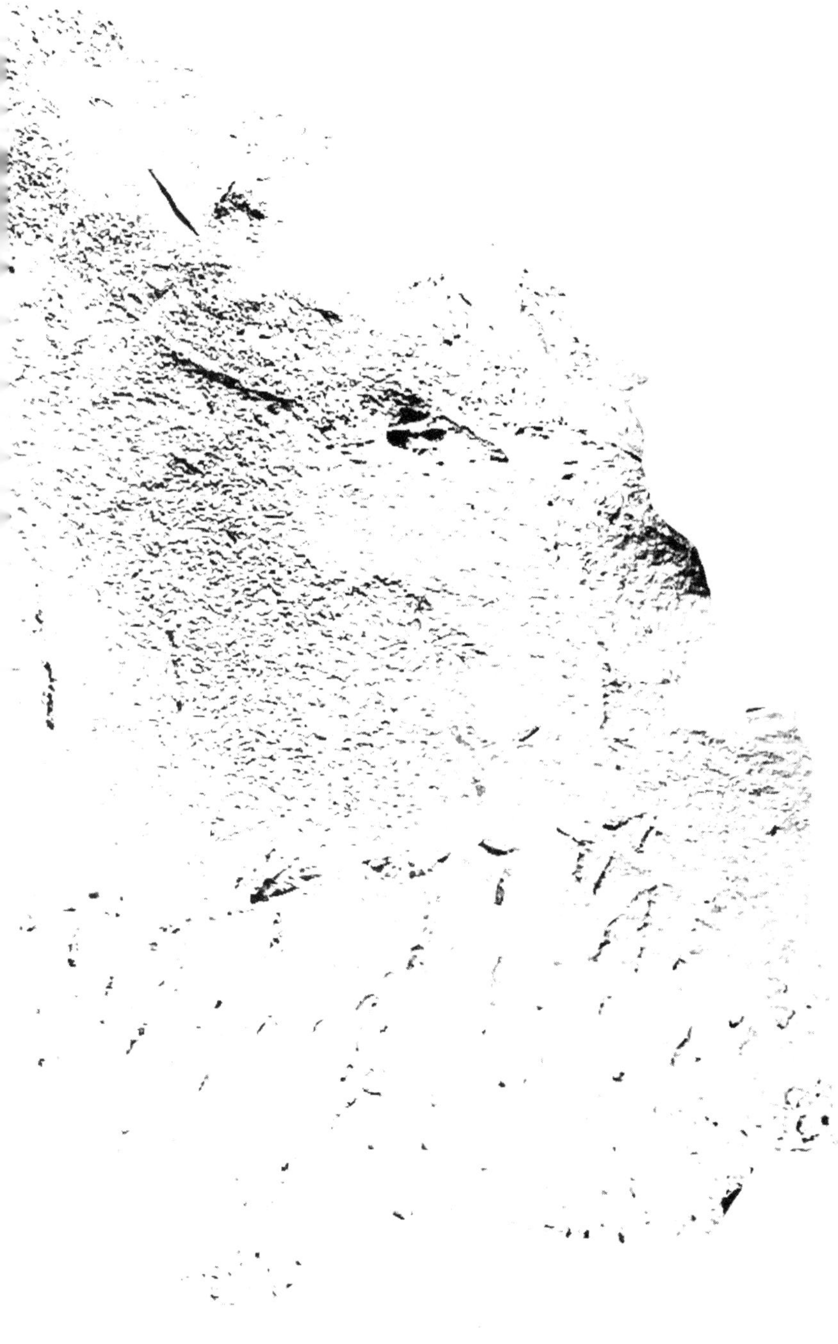